India for the World

India for the World

Ajit Kumar Mahapatra

BLACK EAGLE BOOKS
Dublin, USA | Bhubaneswar, India

🦅 Black Eagle Books
   USA address:
7464 Wisdom Lane
Dublin, OH 43016

India address:
E/312, Trident Galaxy, Kalinga Nagar,
Bhubaneswar-751003, Odisha, India

E-mail: info@blackeaglebooks.org
Website: www.blackeaglebooks.org

First International Edition Published by
Black Eagle Books, 2025

INDIA FOR THE WORLD
by Dr. **Ajit Kumar Mahapatra**

Copyright © Ajit Kumar Mahapatra

All rights reserved. No part of this publication may be reproduced, stored in a retrieval system, or transmitted, in any form or by any means, electronic, mechanical, photocopying, recording or otherwise without the prior permission of the publisher.

Cover & Interior Design: Ezy's Publication

ISBN- 978-1-64560-762-5 (Paperback)

Printed in the United States of America

Dedication

I dedicate this book of poems to my dearest mother whose soul has entered realms in which to be finally freed from prison of material body never to return to this endlessly mutable world of birth, disease, old age and death.
In some shape or other, she always exists to bless me.

Prologue

A lot of things around me – nature, mountains with streaming springs, flowing rivers, animals, people – inspire me. India sees humanity as a joint family. My objective always has been to show to the world that we are the leader of the world and the leading light of the global community.

An anthology of my poems titled **"SEEING THE WORLD"** published in 2024, also in the similar vein highlighted the essence of Indian culture stressing on the foreign policy of peaceful co-existence.

India believes in conscious balancing: neither isolation nor full openness, but managed interdependence. The emerging model of post-global era: not cutting ties, but calibrating connection. India lays adaptive bridges of cooperation. India builds networks, rather than regulations; Atmanirbhar Bharat – India's basic motto.

I was mighty delighted when the 74 years old Alley Mills won "DAYTIME EMMY" award for the second time as guest performer in a daytime drama and its writing team. Alley Mills first won the award in 2023, best known as the mom on "The Wonder Years".

At the Pasadena Civic Auditorium, Alley Mills told the audience: "We are living in really dark times right now. Everything is crazy; we just got to keep our spirits high".

To add to it, Sir David Attenborough makes history at 99. Famed narrator, writer and host becomes the oldest "DAYTIME EMMY" winner for "Secret lives of Orangutans". Van Dyke was 98 when he won as guest performer in a daytime drama series for "DAYS OF OUR LIVES", in 2024. He is also the oldest actor to win a "DAYTIME EMMY". These great personalities are my standard for imitation. Since, I am a senior citizen too, I am also keeping my spirits high to go ahead with my literary journey.

They always inspire me, in lovely pursuit of literary attempts. One more anthology of poems titled **"INDIA FOR THE WORLD"** is ready for publication and launching in November 2025.

Indian customs, festivals, way of life, approaches have been, subtly, assimilated in all of my poems. The readers may cherish; I hope, the readers will appreciate.

Flow of words come into my mind; I cannot resist, I sit on my chair to pen down. I go on writing. Poems are born. May it be in any form; art in any form is ideal. Expression in any form has to be respected.

This is what I have felt in life. Art in any form, and, expression is an art. So also, the literature. It is never doctrinaire. Literature is love. Literature is limitless, it glorifies life, life's events, nature's essence. Life is literature. Life is love.

Therefore, I have learnt to keep my spirit high, to go ahead with love of life and literature.

Ajit Kumar Mahapatra

Foreword

Prof. Prafulla Kumar Mohanty

I was not surprised when Dr. Ajit Kumar Mahapatra called on me, the other day, with a sheaf of typed papers. I could guess the papers were a part of a new book **"INDIA FOR THE WORLD"**. I know Dr. Mahapatra since the last 45 years. He is a versatile genius, well versed in the Arts and Sciences of life. He is a social worker, original thinker and a genial personality. He is innovative, creative and of a helping nature. He is a doctor by profession but a humanist benefactor of the common people by avocation. His presence is inspiring and his enthusiasm is infectious.

Although we met after about 30 years, I felt the fact filling up of the gap of time as he in his usual style poured out his words. He handed over to me the papers, rather the manuscript of his new volume of poems titled as **"India for the World"**. His earlier volume was **"Seeing the World"** and this volume, I thought is a natural follower in his poetic journey.

I always knew Dr. Mahapatra as an innovative person but at first glance I was pleasantly shocked at his audacity. His poems were prose cut into lines of unequal length without the normally accepted attributes of poetry. But as I read along, I started admiring his boldness in creating a new genre. The world has now accepted "Verse Libre". The world has now accepted this new Avatar of poetry after a weak initial resistance. Why not accept now the innovation of Dr. Mahapatra which gives the pleasure of ideas, if not emotions?

Dr. Mahapatra mostly focused on India's varied culture, economic and social traditions and tries to understand the world through India. He appealed to me as a humanist, looking at man's ideas, emotions, behavioural dynamics and the theatrics of "Lila and Moksha". His ideas are morally pure, intellectually honest and temperamentally liberal.

Dr. Mahapatra's world does not reveal the dark forces of anti-life. He understands his total reality as life-friendly. His world is full of joy, festivities and positivity. As an Indian he sees India as a beautiful place where all religions coexist with amity. India is an ancient land with a long history of cultural purity and civilizational excellence. There are thirteen festivals in twelve months – in other words Indian festivals are mass events like Dussera, Rakhi, Kumbha Mela, Deepavali etc. This is because Indian culture believes in relationship. The idea of Basudhaiba Kutumbakam is unique to India. India also believes in eclecticism. Dr. Mahapatra as an inheritor of India's cultural traditions writes with emotional involvement; but an over-seeing critical eye is noticeable in his writing.

Relationship is multifocal. Ajit Mahapatra perceives that this multifocal nature of Indian civilization in the festivals. The festivals are not merely social events, they also are commercial enterprises. The last Kumbha Mela at Prayag Raj is a case in point. Rakhi, Ratha Yatra, the Christmas and other festivals bring people together to display faith as well as holistic well being which includes peace accord, politics and business.

Dr. Mahapatra's understanding of the world is a cognitive experience. He makes men the centre of all human activities. For him life is a multifoliate Rose and this Rose has a symmetry of colour, form and scent. It pleases the senses and also the mind. His view is optimistic. But Dr. Mahapatra suggests a vision which is utopian. He does not bother about the grim realities. I wish man rises above the "sheer absurdities" of the present-day world and accepts life as a perpetual celebration of human goodness.

Dr. Mahapatra envisions world a family in line with India's Basudhaiba Kutumbakam. May his ideas charm the modern mind and transform the world into a Hitler-Trump less abode of peace, harmony, prosperity and plenitude.

Preface: A Reader's Response

Prof. Manmatha Kundu

"Seeing the World" famed Dr. Mahapatra has come up with his second collection of poems "India for the World", continuing his old trend but much mellowed, smoothened and vibrant. He continues the same trend – from local to global- from his native village on the bank of Subarnarekha, close to the sea, close to the village of world-famous writer Manoj Das, to Odisha and then to India, and finally to the world. A globe trotter, rooted in his soil looks at the world at large. He continues the trend of great Indian English poets, Ezekiel, Ramanujan and Odisha's Jayant Mohapatra, Bibhu Padhi and Niranjan Mohanty with a difference. His poems are comprehensible, poems of ideas and intellect with a purpose to change the world. He looks at everything with an objective distance but gets agitated within which gives way to his poems, otherwise all his poems would have been great essays. A cursory look at the content page shows how the titles are in fact titles of essays, be it 'Global

Democracy', 'Human Ingenuity', 'Growth Evenly Balanced', 'World a Family', 'Convergence: India's Mission', or 'Ponds Still Relevant', 'India for the World' (the title of the collection). Is it possible, one wonders, to convert these prose themes into poems? Dr. Mahapatra has made possible the impossible. What made him possible, the impossible? His mastery over words, playing with words, that come to him like 'leaves to trees'. One word flowing into another, then another to another, preceded by flow of ideas following 'Stream of Consciousness'. A few lines from the poem "Ponds Still Relevant", as example, a para conveniently converted into a stanza.

'Marine water bodies
relaxes body and mind,
rejuvenates body functions,
stimulates blood circulation,
flushes out accumulated toxins
reduces water retention
and bloating'

The poem on his village "My Native Village" is very different from other poems, with a deep sense of nostalgia, the unspoiled pastoral beauty and salubrious climate that suit the simple life style of the inhabitants there. The description of the charming pastoral landscape is not found in other poems. It stands apart:

"a plenty of birds gleefully chirping,
crows in groups flying in azure sky,
the early Sun casting a golden glow,
over streaming water of partly full river"

A bit similar to the poem so far, the feeling of nostalgia and the sense of beauty are concerned, is the poem "Confessions" wherein he brings an unusual comparison between the Ganges and the coconut tree, very similar from the religious points of view. The part 4 of the poem is in fact, an extension of his poem on his native village:

"Nostalgia for healthy bath,
swimming with childhood friends,
in the then, deep Subarnarekha"

From his native village he moves to Odisha, his native state, the Capital city Bhubaneswar where he meets a poor helpless woman with 'Sunken Eyes' and then to the western Odisha in "Nuakhai Festival". From there to his much beloved country India, in poems like "Convergence: India's Mission", "India for the World". And finally, from his native village, from his family to the Global Village, the world and 'World a Family'. If one counts the number of poems written on these four themes, his native village, native state, much loved country and the world, the numbers keep on increasing, only one poem on his village but more than six on the world. Dr. Mahapatra's objective seems to change the world; his global village, the 'World a Family' but his much loved country India remains the epicentre, and hence the title of his book "India For the World", Mr. Modi's vision "India to become the Vishwa Guru", and all his poems, be it on his native village, the four poems on festivals – Rakhi, Holi, Christmas and Nuakhai, the poem on climate 'Ponds Still Relevant', the poems related to women exploitation, 'Gender

Bias', 'Sex Racket' that send shivers down my spine are steeped in Indian culture and have deep cultural roots, signature of Dr. Mahapatra's scholarship. The current trend in literature, especially fiction, is not fiction as fiction but fact as fiction. Novels, even stories, are based on facts, real life experiences. Before writing a novel, the writers do serious research on the subject over long years. Dr. Mahapatra's poems have similar base studies not written on the spur of the moment but 'recollected' after long 'tranquillity'. No doubt, therefore, his poems are poems of ideas and intellect involving head but they have a 'heart' as well. The best examples are his poems 'The Last Rakhi', 'Sunken Eyes'.

All his poems, more or less, touch the problems of the world, his world family, faces today, be it cultural degeneration, war, climate problem, gender bias or the like and the only solution according to him is love, the binding force, the panacea.

> Love – a kind of gravity,
> sort of mighty energy
> brings humans, animals, all others,
> closer together,
> endearingly unites
> different communities,
> from various walks of life,
> in times of pleasure
> and penury.

CONTENTS

Prologue	07
Foreword	10
Preface: A Reader's Response	13
Revisiting Childhood	18
My Native Village	24
Confession	28
Global Democracy	34
Human Ingenuity	39
Growth Evenly Balanced	44
World A Family	50
Convergence: India's Mission	55
Ponds Still Relevant	61
India For The World	67
Sunken Eyes	73
Nuakhai Festival	77
Christmas In India	83
The Last Rakhi	88
A Holy Dip At The Sangam	93
Holi Revelry	99
Harmonious Whole	104
Gender Bias	109
Sex Racket	115
Empowering Women	120
Acknowledgement	125
Afterword	127

REVISITING CHILDHOOD

A time travel back
to the 60s
when afternoons spent
playing around,
funning, gossiping,
throwing stones at hanging coconuts,
mangoes, ripe at tree-top,
dislodging, then eating.

There's a real sense of community
in rural area,
rhythms of life rejoicing,
life felt slower, less competitive,
intimate, close, cordial.

A ten-year-old boy
navigates childhood,
observes how mother wrestles
with demands of a daughter,
two younger sons,
heeding to the needs of
working husband;
the boy to endure anger
of strict maths teacher,
not keeping home tasks updated,

caned, offended
in presence of friends,
the incident kept hidden
from the parents.

He reminisces
how father's ritual of
bedtime story telling,
soporific and well narrated,
instead of drifting off to sleep
keeps them wide awake,
they hang on to every word.

Mother remains engaged
till late midnight,
she enters late
to take rest.

Mother's plight
full of sacrifices,
divine, God sent.

A mind that has no fear,
capable of expressing
genuine love.

There's love, compassion
in common civic life,
there's simplicity,
moral supports
in rural way of life.

Lush green environs,
clattering river,
golden morning Sun
adorning,
exhilarating moonlit night,
golden setting Sun,
anoint the onlooker's mind
with jollity, thrill and vibes;
onlooker's mind rejuvenated,
mood begins to fly upward
in the miraculous open sky.

Ultramodern complexities,
stressful life styles,
destroy the sanctity,
fairness of natural
flora and fauna,
pleasantries,
of today's rural life
and living.
It's not size of an act
that matters,
purity of intention that elevates.

Ram Krishna Paramhansa
finds the divine
in the destitute,
Vivekananda reminds,
the least work done
for the good of others
awakens divinity within.

Small act done selflessly,
polishes mirror of the Soul,
mother's selfless actions
existentially indispensable,
God can't be everywhere
created mother to represent.

Simplicity of rural communities
binds all with the power of love,
interdependent and happy
are the rural dwellers,
genuine love, trust humility
influencing them in daily life,
mutual respect for each other
not, silent sabotage ever.

During pleasant monsoon,
rain gives a good bang
to the earth,
summer sweat forgotten
rain calls to life,
rain drops on head and body
give rejuvenating bath,
induce children to rejoice,
float paper boats,
fall ill, suffer from fever.
People going on road
with bikes,
stop to wait under tin roofs
of tea stall or beetle shop,
life, thus takes

a memorable turn
farmers walk bare foot
to see if time ripe
for ploughing.

The thing that can't wait
is moving life,
rain too, can't wait
it downpours
in villages,
beginning of monsoon,
melodious,
the young mostly busy,
in merry making,
funning, frolicking
since, the time can't wait
it passes away.

MY NATIVE VILLAGE

Raised in
a riverain village,
located on abundantly fertile,
sand-filled golden bank of
the river Subarnarekha;
its soil hugely productive
producing large quantities of rice,
of different varieties,
an acknowledged rice bowl,
of the state of Odisha.

Ending a brisk morning river walk
on a sand dune – drift of sand-
rested a while to recover strength
inhaling salubrious air,
wind chilling out,
eyes amiable rivetted on
fascinating, picturesque riverscape,
a plenty of birds gleefully chirping,
crows in groups flying in azure sky,
the early Sun casting a golden glow
over streaming water of partly full river,
Flying crows making low hoarse sounds
roused the sleeping inhabitants,
sleep fresh from previous night's slumber,

large plumaged black crow
 reminded of quill pens we used
for fine writing during school days,
the pens made of quill of a crow.

Morning hour's soothing Sunshine
magnificently illumined
lustrous apex of "Bhairava" temple,
umbrageous astonishing mango leaves,
tall coconut trees, luscious banana plants,
lush green wide field
surrounding the village temple,
always would mesmerise all on earth,
the humans, animals and plants
for, all they are intertwined,
interconnected at sub-atomic stage.

There existed a few old
humbling mud houses
with thatch roofs,
simple architectural marvel,
stood as an example of negotiation
between nature, tradition, modernity,
the mud houses, cool, hygienic from within.

In this memorable native home
our family grew together,
shared with family and friends,
happily could stay and relax,
could be at ease;
every clatter, every Sunrise, setting Sun

every bird chirping, luscious fruit,
silvery river Subarnarekha,
all significantly point out to nature's magic;
when asked about my sweet lovely home
I thought about my closest friends,
unforgettable moments spent with them,
ephemeral mind-bending times
with the nearest relatives,
and exhilarating songs that travelled with me.

My native village now changing shape
morphing into a "known-unknown",
with structural, economic implications
for the global order;
women, here, remain underutilized
in growing economy,
women face significant barrier
ironically at home;
violence at home impacts
future generation.

Safety and dignity of every woman,
to be prioritised in every family,
not in policy, also in practice,
the state of Odisha in India
actively scouting potential locations
to bring the vision to life,
to become an inclusive
and developed economy.

(1)
Mighty river holy Ganges
I revere and trust the most,
a life line for millions,
across South Asia.

Climate change, shifting monsoons,
relentless extractions, damming up,
all human inducible,
push up the holiest river
towards collapse.

The sustaining, enduring Ganges,
dries up faster than
ever before.

Birth of mother "Ganga",
in dynamic course of
nature's evolutionary process,
an eventful manifestation;
no involvement, no interference
whatsoever, of any
human endeavour.

Therefore, functionally
dependable, logical,
impartial and inclusive,
hurting none, depriving none,
embracing all.

Sitting on my heels
on healing bank of Ganga
with knees drawn up,
folded hands, I bow down
to express gratitude
before mother Ganga,
for selfless motherly love,
healing care, nourishment.

The river and its tributaries
nurtured over
six hundred fifty million people.

A densely populated region
banks upon its fresh water,
food, economic advantages.

Alas! its decline accelerates,
beyond anything seen,
in recorded history.

(2)
Also, I respect, and trust
hilarious coconut tree,
with unbranched stem,

crown of large,
fan-shaped leaves,
leaf of this,
a symbol of victory.

Coconut containing edible kernel,
enclosing milky juice,
not only nutritious,
milky juice quenches thirst,
delicious white kernel
lessens extent of hunger,
satisfies, cools down temper,
during hot summer days.

In Hindu tradition,
green coconut cleaned,
kept on top of earthen vessel
at the time of worship,
not only essential, indispensable,
green coconut with,
divine component.

Coconut tree never betrays,
edible nuts commercially used,
yields coconut butter,
coconut oil, coconut milk;
coconut ice – a kind of sweet,
of coconut and sugar,
coconut mat – made of husk
of coconut.

Coconut tree
not of human creation,
integrating part of
complex universe,
most dependable,
doubtless trustworthy.

(3)
Propaganda paradox:
deception of modern politics
impels one to disbelieve
modern brand of politicians;
politics wouldn't leave us,
in a dynamic democracy
every individual vote counts,
politicians, depend on people
for their survival.

In modern party politics,
the politicians tend to strive
more for the benefit of party,
barring a few distinguished politicians
who put priority on development,
transcending caste bias,
religion, location.

Statesmen/Stateswomen
have to be relied on,
they're charismatic leaders,
dependable, trustworthy,
adorable.

(4)
Born, raised
as a riverside dweller,
brought up in the midst of
riverain simplicity,
traditional customs,
since childhood,
running, playing, jumping
in soothing lap of nature,
the minuscule river bank,
exciting palm beach;
obsessed with
bountiful nature
and environment.

Nostalgic for healthy bath,
swimming, with childhood friends,
in the then, deep Subarnarekha.

Hugely fond of
the riverside village,
now, transforming fast,
entices me till today;
the golden sandy beach,
flying, chirping colourful bird's,
grassy fertile green field,
flowing, cluttering Subarnarekha.

Simplicity, trustworthiness,
inclusivity, love, compassion,
selfless service to the humanity,
always, to my liking.

Global military expenses
meanwhile surged,
foreign aid-budgets
instantaneously reduced,
dehumanising disruptive tendencies
gaining ground,
mercilessly penetrate into
vulnerable human minds
eroding love, trust,
compassion, brotherhood,
collapsing civilization.

Wealthy country's aid-budget
played vital roles:
supported job creation
promoted industrial growth,
declined where it was
needed most.

World's poorest population
increasingly drowned out,
hyper-nationalism
in advanced economies
rising at the risk of
deteriorating conditions
across developing world.

Growing number of migrants
prefer going to
wealthier nations
to up financial status.

Mentality of
mutual cooperation
on the low,
azure sky gets dusted
with hopeless clouds;
despite such
lacklustre environment,
the Sun shines,
sunrays bright
transforming and bringing
human minds,
back to nascent pure form,
to reform rules of
multilateral engagements,

as top priority,
to strengthen
global democracy.

Civil society organisations,
the governments to ponder
around shared objectives,
striving towards world unity,
welfare of humanity.

Awakened souls,
in the process of evolution,

transformed into
super human beings.

Voice of developing economies
emerging nations
in multilateral negotiations
subdued, depending on
financial contributions.

Voting power allocated
to members of world bodies,
International Monetary fund,
the World Bank,
depends on
financial contributions,
striking disparity
fundamentally betraying
democratic principles.

India's secular democracy
the world's largest one,
co-founder of
non-alignment movement,
over last few years
India aligned with
Trump's foreign policy,
erodes its global standing;
eight years after,
India's independence,
in Bandung Conference (Indonesia),
a broad coalition of countries

brought closer together,
India's role being unique.

Coalition of countries refused
to remain in shadows of
dominant powers.

Human hearts to govern,
love has to rule,
in international dialogues,
non-violence to transform
mindsets of world leaders,
their decisions to be
humancentric, positive,
to build a better world.

Rising nationalism,
geo-political fragmentation,
retreat from
multilateral cooperations
lead to a fractured world;
has to be healed
to promote global democracy,
for welfare of humanity.

To revitalize democratic governance,
to restore dignity of
marginalised communities,
to protect rights of those
who will inherit the planet.

HUMAN INGENUITY

With unusually great ability to move,
to seek out avenues of adapting
to altogether altered situations,
conscious life comes alive through
continuing to exist, to survive
on this planet earth;
characteristically life adapts, life evolves,
prevailing circumstances,
around all of us do alter.

Million years ago
unique earth's temperature ranged
between six hundred
and twelve hundred degrees Celsius,
its surface replete with
noxious substances, air toxic,
wondrous life adapted to,
also survived,
on this kind earth.
Ingenious life knows to accommodate,
to unfold, continuing to exist.

Evolution found to follow
geopolitical time frame,

queer pattern of human life
a biological process;
human brain and body
tend to mutate into
something more sophisticated,
more refined, moving towards
a better form of adaptation
resulting in change of lifestyle
along with multiplication of human wants;
the world moves too fast,
the grand evolution has been
useful in real sense.

Despite tremendous technological advances
yet to ascertain all that the earth contains,
It seems extremely difficult to measure
availability of all its resources.

The doomsters caution, the world faces
depleting resources,
global population swells
crossing eight billion now
India's population overtakes China's,
frightened millions
warn of impending scarcity,
an environmental apocalypse,
the contrary is ground reality.

The human life expectancy
has considerably increased,
per capita consumption skyrocketed,

commodities more abundant,
cheaper in real term;
a smart phone replaces
landline, newspapers, television,
camera, a lot of other items;
the ground reality joyfully heralds
"more from less".

Every percentage increase
in earth's population,
global resource abundance increase
eight times higher;
people not a burden on
rather, creators of resources.

Economist Julian Simon confirms,
"human ingenuity, the greatest resource,
not land, food, or minerals"
More people the world has

More the number of creative brains,
More group experiments,
More specialisation,
all reducing "cost" remarkably.

To quote from the book, "Superabundance"
"abundance is rising
four percent per year
much faster than population".

Humans are prone to make errors,
rising income may create problems.
high consumption involves
environmental side effects;
truer still, more brain power,
and human ingenuity,
more the possibility of
solution of consequent problems.

World needs, not fewer humans,
needs more introspection,
more innovation, more careful analysis.

Population control
a moral, and economic issue
It ought to be voluntary
never by arbitrary use
of authority.

Money, the visible sign of strength
energises one's body and mind
propels one to traverse the runway
to reach cherished destination.
In an age of digital technology
strategic use of artificial intelligence
money having inherent force matters.

The advantaged prefer to host
a thriving business ecosystem
as in other spheres
so, in that of making money
a few, specially gifted, can earn
much more than they actually need.

Following grand principle of Trusteeship
those blessed with plenty
may share excess wealth,
if they so like, with
those at a disadvantage,
who make their way with difficulty.

Dignified attitude of sharing with others,
standing behind someone during distress

are divine moments,
lived by a lucky one;
takes place when one's thoughts,
not guided by separative ego
but, by unifying force of love
rooted in a sense of oneness.

Political, economic, inclusive institutions
focus on sustained economic growth,
extractive institutions impoverish nations
with poor, negative rule of law.

It's only institutions,
that determine a nation's future.
Humans are bound to try and save
Our planet in crisis;
A country, to ensure wellbeing of its citizens
Needs to grow its economy,
to raise, its GDP.
The total value of goods and services
produced within the country, called GDP.

American economist Simon Kuznets,
developed the national income statistics, in 1934,
GDP – the key measure
of a country's economic progress.

Adoption of market led economy
benefitted those who have money
who have buying power,
not the unprivileged millions,

forced to live with scarcity
to make both ends meet.

GDP – the key measure widely adopted,
willing or coerced, found to be
a narrow measure of welfare,
ignoring wellbeing of humans
and the planet earth.

"Goods and services" production
requires energy, causing
green-house gas emission,
increasing GDP translates
directly to increasing emission.

The nations stress on amassing
material resources,
power acquisition, short term goals,
driven by narrow self-interests
contributing to socio-environmental crises,

measuring progress against each other
in monetary terms,
do care about money,
less about caring for each other.

Being obsessive about GDP growth
for huge material gain
one drifts towards advanced infrastructure,
monetary progress, material comforts
leads to a fragmented view of reality

ignoring wellbeing of humans,
and the planet, in its entirety;
with this partial rationality
one fails to perceive deeper connections
the inherent wholeness
of universal mechanism.

It's a vital societal issue.
This imbalance manifests
as social disintegration,
existential threats, environmental degradation.

Global order unravelling
supremacy of power struggle
sought to be established
on the battle ground,
international laws violated,
the world watches, the leaders
have scant regards for sanctity
of human life, and living
causing blatant erosion of human value.

Just has to be growth pattern,
facilitating uniform material advance,
not uneven amelioration
benefitting minuscule few.
Growth with lower intensity
energy-use, alleviates poverty
faster, the research shows;
The world has to explore,

find an alternative better "measure"
of material progress,
a different inclusive pathway
of "even economic growth"
towards universal human wellbeing.

The world has to have individuals
not just cognitively adept
also, emotionally, and spiritually balanced.

Happiness, dependent not on material conditions,
fundamentally more in mind and soul.

From Egypt to the Indus
civilisations evolved near rivers,
earth's water enabled productive farming,
growing crops, rearing animals,
nurturing agriculture, supporting natural world,
nourishing the humanity generously.

Water resource created
since origin of universe
to the evolution of humanity.
Humans, then constructed
water supply structures,
learnt to purify and provide
safe drinking water.

Big dams, reservoirs, subsequently built
catering to increasing demands
of life sustaining essential water.
Water played its important role
in emerging first great civilisations;
civilisations in India,
the Middle East, and China.

Ancient Mesopotamia endeavoured
drafting of the first waterlaws,
The "Code of Hammurabi",
crafted around 1700 B.C.
granted the highest status
to the industrious farmers
who aptly managed precious water
with productive farming.

To subsist in the Universe,
availability of water matters,
to the communities, cities,
corporate houses, downstream areas.
Water obeys no boundaries,
knows no nation, no borders,
Major rivers, from those in India
to the Amazon, the Mississippi,
shared by two or more nations;
there, the citizens, help harmonise
bonding with sustainable nature.

"Wyland Icon Award" winner,
celebrated marine film maker,
"Jill Heinerth", confessed her bonding
with marine ecosystems, the world of water;
she expressed, "felt extremely privileged
to swim through veins of Mother Earth
in the life blood of our planet;
it's no accident that tears, the Ocean,
the amniotic fluid are the same."
Water planet is the cradle of life.

Earth has seventy percent water,
Human body contains seventy percent water,
Azure ocean enables
one out of every two breaths,
functioning as lungs of the planet
vindicating systemic interconnectivity.

Humanity soberly accepts
"We are global citizens"
India asserts, "world is one family",
actions, all we perform
effect others instantly;
everything done on land surface
returned to us to drink;
the effects of pollution
soaked into the ground
distributed into
spread out water bodies.

The Pacific Ocean is crying of
a plastic garbage patch
twice the size of Texas;
sea birds perish from plastic ingestion,
plastic pollution degrades
stunning coral island reef,
detrimentally affecting marine species.

Human activity has repercussion
all the way across space;
global lockdowns, scientists infer,
affected faraway moon

pushed its temperature down;
Human activity changed climate on earth
turned waterbodies into poison,
drove live species to extinction.

A world family
built on exploitation
surely will crumble
beneath the burden
of its own weight;
a family to be built
in a spirit of endearment;
one should encroach on
no one's rights,
no one's place of belonging.

CONVERGENCE: INDIA'S MISSION

Multi-ideological, world
global powers at loggerheads,
in the throes of war,
multi-dimensional,
multi-locational,
all for ideological differences.

Warring nations
deem it just and fair,
since, they fight for a cause.

I made a moment's pause,
went into the very root of
an irony:
universe wonderfully crafted,
just one,
shelter giving earth
created as one,
ingenious human race
solitary one,
human species - a single
homogeneous class of
living being,
all interconnected

at sub-atomic stage;
evolving individuals,
discern the good
from the bad,
the moral, from the immoral,
intend whole heartedly
to stay in peace,
for harmonious living,
for better progress,
ostentatious prosperity.

Driven by instincts of
greed, lust, arrogance
people bound to disrupt peace,
law, order, harmony;
consequently, wars erupt,
witnessing disastrous bloodshed,
catastrophic wars tell
sordid stories of
death, destruction,
both camps suffer,
of the victor,
of the vanquished.

Digital modern warfare
multi-dimensional,
of kinetic, cyber, economic;
destructive effects in one location
inevitably spill over to
other localities.

Divided and splintered,
forward motion of growth,
internal development process
of growing nations,
get crippled,
pragmatic convergence,
the only solution,
ultimately focussing on
practicable notion of
harmonious coexistence;
shared experience of
sustainable socio-cultural growth
wedded to
embracing idea of equality.

Harmony in diversity
eagerly pays attention to others,
encourages to appreciate
others' way of life,
joyously celebrates
love fully being in "Weness".
No matter,
Whatever be the differences,
in background,
cultures, religious faiths,
without being judgemental,
love connects all together,
Love – a kind of gravity,
sort of mighty energy,
brings humans, animals, all others,
closer together,

endearingly unites
different communities,
from various walks of life
in times of pleasure
and penury.

Love diminishes
obstructive boundaries,
functions as a common thread,
weaves all together,
in a society,
a nation, at large.
May be slow,
world events
seen gradually drift towards
unity of mankind,
tending initially to
fusion of different cultures,
for a brighter, nobler life,
for whole of mankind.

In particular,
for fast evolving India,
I harbour an exclusive dream:
in its evolution upwards
Indians would be raised to
a higher larger consciousness,
then as perfect individuals,
would guide the humanity.

Early in the morning I got up,
thought of what a lovely divine grace
it was to be healthily alive -
to inhale, to laugh, to love, to enjoy.
The impact of Indian culture.

Ancient Indian temples
normally accompany
water bodies with,
small or big,
depending on
availability of space,
adjacent to
or a small distance away;
presiding deities
reverently reside in
enormously built
excellent massive temples,
onlookers astounded on seeing
mute presence of
unparalleled pristine
architectural marvel
on the golden bank of
flowing rivers, or ashore
sacred oceans.

Roots of temple sites
linked with
mythological divine episodes
described in inscriptions

for wider public inspection
depicted in legends
of Hinduism.

Visitors seeking entry
into "Garbha Griha"
for performance of customary puja
have to adhere to purifying
ritualistic norms,
have to have a full body bath
in adjoining pond,
therefore, the pond,
prior to touching holy deities
seated inside the sacred
"Garbha Griha".

Traditional customs demand
mandatory construction of
adjoining water body,
simultaneous with
construction of temple,
to comply with
ancient religious rules.

Conventional aquatic healing
with its hoary efficacious past
given its rightful place
in humanising Indian way of life,
spiritually co-ordinated
healthfully integrated,
scientifically advanced.

Anupam Mishra's book
'Aaj Bhi Khare Hain Talab'
(the ponds are still relevant)
a holy book for water warriors,
continues to usher in
fundamental change
"one pond at a time"
quietly sparked a revolution
in water conservation
across villages.

The book helped mobilize,
build awareness around,
check-dams, and ponds;
desert area – Jaisalmer district
restored about five hundred
ponds, wells, and beris,
(beri – shallow well)
global water shortage
an impending reality.

Kumbha Mela – a holy dip in Sangam,
a mineral rich marine health care
spiritually practised in India,
to attract all to join;
healing touch of the blue sea
for ever eternal.

Mineral rich marine healthcare
a rich legacy,
to address modern day ailments.

Legendary Queen Cleopatra
indulged in water baths,
water infused with
rose petals, raw milk,
for skin care, therapeutic uses.

Temple water bodies
Indians revere
for divine value,
therapeutic usefulness.

Marine water bath
relaxes body and mind,
rejuvenates body functions,
stimulates blood circulation,
flushes out accumulated toxins,
reduces water retention
and bloating.

The Greeks believe,
Aphrodite – the goddess of
love and beauty,
rose fully formed
from the sea foam.

Blend of science,
recuperative nature,
feels relevant for humans
seeking holistic health,
to address weariness, stress,
skin infections.

Water is the key
to a radiant complexion
indigenous water wisdom
scattered across the country,
the ponds, there, ensure
a cool weather.

INDIA FOR THE WORLD

In the doctrine of war
the suffering of an enemy
is no suffering;
those doing the killing
are indifferent to
the suffering of the other.

Government keeps an army
either for the country's defence
or for fulfilling the longing
for conquest.

The outcome of war
is more war,
modern technology,
advanced weaponry,
being profusely misused,
have enormously increased
the chances of provocations,
chaotic disruptions,
causing bloodshed, mass slaughter
driving to cosmic meaninglessness.

The war always brings
the end of empathy,

kills spirituality,
deadens the soul.

The nation that chooses to rise
faces chaos with clarity of vision,
builds ideologies based on
love, nonviolence, compassion,
staying far away from
hate, violence, authoritativeness.

Global responsibility
not just to wield power
it's about building infrastructures
for the welfare of humankind,
manifesting positive unifying force

to unify the splinter group,
displaying political maturity
while dealing with world political issues,
and rewriting
the destiny of the universe.

Materialistic approach of
governance and development,
will have downfall
at some point of time,
a nation's spiritual clarity
is its strength,
its strategy,
and quiet dominance with depth.

India rises,
holds key to global greatness,
no amount of hostility
can stop India,
India looks forward unshaken,
looks up with resilience,
India evolves fast,
faster than many other countries.

India is a quiet power,
it doesn't shout,
India is confident, self-reliant,
India stresses on its youth force,
on youth digital empowerment,
India' s ideology based on
love, nonviolence, inclusivity,
unity in diversity,
India internationally not isolated,
its lifestyle
rooted in science,
rooted in the concept of
sustainability,
India's advancement,
is its spiritual clarity.

Indian thinkers and scientists,
having come across,
devastating incidents of
excesses of brutality, mass rapes,
during Bangladesh Liberation war,
mass children's graves in Gaza,

got shocked unexpectedly,
shouted "collapse of civilization"
against the natural order;
its ripples of trauma
touched their families.

Aurobindo with Mirra Alfassa,
his French spiritual collaborator,
founded "Aurobindo Ashram",
exactly a century back in India,
known as "Auroville",
three hours drive south from Chennai,
in the Union Territory of Puducherry.
It's an experimental community
based on human unity.

Seven decades ago,
a group of Europeans built
a universal collective township,
the one, that belonged to humanity,
not to any individual, or government,
the residents united by
Shri Aurobindo's principles of
unity in diversity,
the barren land turned into
a lush green sustainable township.

Creation of Auroville
was for achieving human unity,
being away from contending religions,
national rivalries,

men can happily live
not being mired in

controversies, and contradictions.
The assimilation of cultures
through cultural exchanges,
collaborative ventures
Auroville like community living,
enriches the sense of
a peaceful community life.

Application of non-violence
in international governance,
role of love
in international dialogue,
are the only effective steps
to halt disruptions, disorders,
and hazardous war,
the outcome of love
is more love,
the outcome of peace
is more peace.

At Rajmahal Square
alighted from urban transport bus,
got sight of a lady,
body emaciated,
clean dressed,
eyes sunken,
cheeks shrunk,
above fifty years of age,
asking for help, might be,
a meagre sum of money;
a mellowed moment indeed,
I paused for a while,
it was a very hot afternoon.

I took out water bottle
from hand bag carried with,
lovingly handed over to her,
requesting politely to drink
to quench her thirst,
that was her existential need,
a necessity for her body
during hot hour;
stretching out the right hand
she took the bottle from me,
corked it out, drank water

gladly, very eagerly,
a small bottle, she emptied
after a few sips,
all the time looking at me
silently, but thoughtfully.

Close by, there a pavement hotel
I took her to,
ordinary local food
the hotel boy served her
on my order,
that too, cheerfully she consumed;
bill paid, both of us
came out of the hotel.

To my amazement
the lady, suddenly stopped me,
kept her trembling right palm
on my head, and uttered,
"live long, enjoy till ripe old age",
she returned to her normal self
of simplicity, loveliness
her face glowing,
she expressed gratitude
in an "Indian way" to me.
Abject poverty didn't
rob her of
her sense of gratitude,
womanly, loving, caring heart.

Blessings rained
from her heart

spontaneously,
that couldn't be bought
couldn't be earned;
Blessings linked with
good works done,
which never went in vain,
always emotionally impacted
the good doers, in profusion.

Seniors, in twilight of life
to keep their spirits high,
to navigate life's challenges,
to suffer less, thrive better,
find creative ways
to deal with life's issues,
may follow the concept of "Joy Span"
promoted for the welfare of mankind
by Kerry Burnight,
former Professor of Medicine,
University of California.

How meticulously
one navigates ups and downs
gives the difference between
"thriving, and suffering"
that's what
"Joy Span" is all about,
to keep spirits up,
find joy in later life
concept of Joy Span
is the panacea.

A year's persistent effort
yields success in academic exam,
aims accomplished
students, hugely relaxed,
plan out rejoicing
the interim period
to heart's content;
the toiling farmers
laborious peasants
tend to unwind,
chill out leisurely
having acquired
abounding harvest of crops.

Burdened self
to be back to normalcy,
humans instinctively
tend to cooldown,
being at leisure
in its therapeutic effects.

Nuakhai – popular agrarian ritual,
the harmony of harvest,

festival of reunion,
ideal time to jubilantly delight
celebrated by gregarious
lovely people of Western Odisha.

Since ages, ceremonially observed,
a quiet tradition, divine practice
of loving, greeting, gifting, sharing;
heads bowing down
before the presiding deity,
expressing heartfelt gratitude,
together with family, friends, invitees.

Dancing, singing, praying
expressing thanks to mother earth,
for year's successful harvest.

The ritual offers insight into
pristine heritage, rich tradition,
cultural excellence,
enviably shaping social fabric of
fertile western region of Odisha.

Nuakhai delves deep into
Vedic origin of
"Pralambana Yajna"
The first crop cutting ceremony.

The founder of Patna state
Raja Ramai Deo, in 14th century
initiated the ritual

ideally to boost economy,
social harmony.

Western Odisha diaspora
across India and abroad
religiously observe Nuakhai
on the fifth of "Bhadrava",
"Sukla Pakshya", day following
Ganesha Chathurthi.

Presiding deity Samaleswari
spruced up, decorated
with vermilion, ornaments, saree,
mighty seductive to look.

"Lagna" – auspicious time fixed
to offer "nabanna" – new rice
to Goddess Samaleswari
the ritual reminds,
surrender of self,
while expressing gratitude,
to presiding deity
for plentiful harvest.

People clean, decorate homes
courtyards, walls adorned
with "Jhoti" – designs, patterns,
made of rice paste on surface.

Indispensable component
"Adhia" – much more than

mere symbolic gift,
involves presenting
food grains, pulses,
vegetables, new clothes
to domestic employees
and neighbours,
no household in community
to be left out.

The eldest in a family
leads the ceremony
of rice offering to deity,
distribution of blessed rice,
to everyone
assembled at venue.

Whole family eats together,
mutton curry, kheeri,
snacks, sweets,
rice dal, remain favourites.

"Nuakhai Juhar" – important custom
ensues, people greet each other,
exchange good wishes;
girls perform folk dances,
"Dalkhai, Rasarkeli, Bajnia,
Machnia" – to the beats of
traditional drums; dhol, tassa,
nisan, with "Sambalpuri Music".

Hard labour of the farmers
eulogized, honoured, having shared
enchanting common culture,
sense of belonging
of a loving community.

Food providing peasants, farmers,
do deserve primacy,
social dignity, love, compassion;
Nuakhai – a fit occasion
for the farmers, and peasants,
worthy of getting gratefulness
from the young, the old alike.

In India Hindus
endearingly observe
Merry Christmas
in celebration of
the birth of Christ,
held on 25 December
every year,
in a culture
that reverently celebrates
the birth of a holy child, Krishna,
advent of another
holy child, Jesus,
fits right in
with liberal, loving
Hindu sentiment.

India – World's oldest peace-keeper
surging ahead with
youthful vibrancy
towards global growth,
universal peace, brotherhood,
love and compassion
reigning supreme.

In northern states of India
Christmas has become
a Hindu festival
pompously performed
in Hindu houses.

Christmas tree – a tree setup
in a room or a public place,
decorated with lights, gifts
at Christmas time,
Christmas cake – a fruit rich
Cake, usually iced,
Christmas pudding – a rich,
spicy fruit, pudding,
Santa hats, hugely popular with
Hindu families
who freely participate
enjoying different traditions
with liberty, without fear.

There was once, a Jewish man
who taught, "God is Love"
to large crowd of people
who congregated to hear him,
was cruelly punished
for saying so;
a cult grew, later on,
in his name,
evolved into a major
world religion - the Christianity.

"God is Love" resonates well
with Hindu perceptions of God
as most loving, caring
compassionate entity.

With a loving picture of
Mother Mary, holding a lovely baby,
lovingly kept
against the wall of a room
for all to see
join the festive fascinating festival
feasting on fruit rich
Christmas cake,
spicy Christmas pudding,
playing the piano
singing carols joyfully,
singing joyous Christmas hymns
happy Christmas celebrated
with charming traditions
in India too,
by both Christians, and Hindus.

Exaltation of music
the most ideal way
of expressing devotion to God,
composer Johannes Bach
famously expressed,
"the noblest music was
that in praise of God"

Music, expression of
love and beauty,
Music is love, music is divine,
Music dispels sadness,
generates beauty,
Music cures ailments,
Promotes wellness,
Music doesn't discriminate,
it invites, doesn't divide,
promotes bonding.
Music opens gateways,
to godliness, peaceful environment.

Humanitarian services
to the needly,
to the marginalised,
to the poor,
most pleasing to God,
service to men is service to God,
all faiths wholly agree on
humanitarian services,
Jesus came as promised messiah
to save the sinners

through his own death.
Christmas unites, invites all
fostering friendship and goodwill,
opens doors to human unity,
collective, human living,
leading to enduring, human bonding.

THE LAST RAKHI

The Indian ritual
Raksha Bandhan
reaffirms bonding
between a sister
and her brother;
parents lovingly welcome
sanctimonious day
as celebration of attachment
and defence from
extraneous oppositions.

On the full moon day
of Sravan,
the sister ties Rakhi: thread bracelet
to right wrist
of her brother,
reminding congenital ties
that hold them together,
despite apparent fragmentations
of present-day
family patterns.

Hindu religious ritual
of a sister's tying Rakhi

to somebody
considered as brother,
is a profound celebration
of human connection,
reaffirming natural attraction,
connectedness
and reciprocal reaction.

Festival's roots stretch
deep into mythological history.

Draupadi tore her sari
to bind Krishna's bleeding finger,
Krishna reciprocated,
rescued sister Draupadi's
unblemished reputation
in her darkest hour.

Also recounts one more episode,
seeking defence
against invaders
Karnavati, the Queen of Mewar
dispatched Rakhi
to Mughal Emperor Humayun,
Humayun, in return,
rushed to Karnavati's aid
elevating idea of
brotherly duty.

Festival's divine depth,
rediscovers eternal value

of India's familial love,
attachment – the kind that asks
for no reason, no reward.

Current year's Rakhi Bandhan
turned sour,
Whatsapp message
from a friend
I received,
on hectic morning
of colourful festive day;
in Krishtapuram village
of Hyderabad's

Kusumanchi Mandal,
25 years old
Pandiri Appireddy's
family members,
busy in preparing
lovely festive events,
Appireddy's sister
readying for
the divine custom,
indisposed for
a few days,
Pandiri Appireddy
breathed his last,
to everybody's shock
those around,
moved to tears,
silence broken,

by sobs, prayers,
Appireddy's sister,
dressed in
a simple sari,
tears streamed
down her face,
hands trembling,
approached her
brother's bier;
she tied a Rakhi
to deceased brother's wrist

to celebrate,
the eternal bond
between the two,
bidding him a tragic
final farewell,
life is fragile.

Shaken sister's last Rakhi
tied with love, grief,
unbreakable memory,
left the entire village
in tears.

A HOLY DIP AT THE SANGAM

Devoutness, and fervency that
Stunningly drew multitude of people
from every corner of
magnificent homeland, Bharat,
to the holy banks of
venerable Triveni Sangam,
with exclusive purpose of
having a holy dip
in divine Sangam,
hallowed confluence of rivers
the Ganga, Yamuna and Saraswati.
And, holding in possession
the rarest feeling of heavenly bliss
of having taken divine dip
in the sacred water of
purificatory Triveni Sangam.

Immersed in a sea of millions
on this wondrous spiritual journey,
impelled to jostle, push at every step
virtually got stupefied, and witnessed,
children clinging to their parents,
elders perched on younger shoulders
in the midst of human tide,

stark reality of a pilgrimage
of huge magnitude.

Only, faith, human determination,
the sacred beckon of spiritual Sangam
drove millions of spirited pilgrims
to the world's largest
spiritual congregation of
Hindu faith, Hindu Tradition
divinizing, purifying,
fervent human souls;
the strangers became friends
with one another, sharing
whatever they had with them,
children passing from hand to hand
whoever the elders approached
all being voluntarily escorted
to the designated place
on reaching the water's edge.

I witnessed,
the most incredible sight of
Sadhus assembled in thousands,
their bodies painted with
vermillion and ash,
wading into sacred water of,
inviting, embracing, Triveni Sangam;
being in communion with
their spirituality; their faces
radiating heartfelt joy and jubilation
after the, most desired divine dip.

Taking a dip in
Triveni Sangam
during Mahakumbha festival,
considered ostentatiously pious,
thus, opine the Hindu believers,
symbolic of purification of soul.

Immersing in holy waters
also, a Christian tradition
of purification of body, and soul;
Jesus was baptised by John
in water of the river Jordan,
Baptism: an immersion into
the Paschal Mystery,
celebrated at Easter;
Christian discipleship
precisely is the call
of leaving 'the Self" behind.

When one tries to help others
one finds ways to God;
living a religious way of life,
one has to have
a compassionate loving heart
leaving "the Self" far behind.

The sacred water of holy
Triveni Sangam,
collected in bottles for
auspicious customary use
that the pilgrims brought back

became a precious commodity
tinged with divine bliss
for all Hindu believers.

Quick commerce platforms
began dipping their feet
into the commercial business
turning sacred Sangam Water
into a marketable commodity
both at home in India
and abroad,
Hindu followers staying abroad
do use the holy water
for auspicious ceremonies,
baby birth, house warming rituals.

Thus, asserts the mammoth gathering
how strong one may be
one, found to cultivate
the team spirit,
to achieve all round success;
when one collaborates,
experiences,
the magic of synergy,
collective efforts far exceed
the sum of individual contribution
inclusivity matters.

The international order transitions
from a unipolar world
to a multipolar universe.

Co-operative multilateralism
only would ensure
peaceful global governance;
international co-ordination
on shared global problems
would protect biodiversity,
accelerate world economic growth
leading to a peaceful
unified multipolar universe.

On dazzling bright, full moon night
of enormously festive month of "Phalguna",
"Holika Dahan" bonfires delightfully lit
across India, resplendent with
diverse cultures, multiple customs
handed down to posterity, since ages.

With family, friends assembled around
Endearingly throwing green grams, sesame seeds,
Potatoes, brinjals, wheat into open fires,
The ravellers reposing unflinching faith
in the ancient Indian customs
of burning bonfires, bearing a bold mission
of triumph of good over evil.

It's more than mere manifest
revelry of colours,
hilarious observance of burning bonfires,
traditionally extolled, bidding welcome to
advent of salubrious spring
into wonderful country, Bharat;
gratefully expressing goodbye at parting
of winter time, hoping to have
an affluent, abundant life on Earth.

Holika Dahan the divine customary ritual,
believed to incinerate inner faults,
transforming one's self to a new stage of
purified, "no-self" stage: a rejuvenated,
higher level of consciousness.

On the eve of Holi revelry
Holika Dahan collectively observed,
Vividly described in Sanskrit Play "Ratnavali",
attributed to King of Kannauj,
Harshbardhan. (606-647 CE)
Bonfire flames blaze up, not just to

burn material offering, wood and straw
but, to incinerate bundle of vices,
dissolving human ego, lust and greed,
authoritatively imposing of ideas on others,
helping create conducive ground
for communal harmony,
making mother earth's sustaining soil,
abundantly productive, and bounteous.

"Holika", King Hiranya Kashyap's sister
stepped into violent flames,
to satiate her brother, with his son
Prahlad, adorer of Vishnu,
Holika got burnt to ashes,
Prahlad, saved, instead;
Arrogant Hiranya Kashyap despised
Lord Vishnu, hence, son Prahlad.

Vishnu as Narasimha, half man, half lion,
killed Hiranya Kashyap, the arrogant king,
on the doorstep at dusk.

The one without love and compassion
grows narcissistic and closed,
how much can one know himself
without knowing the others,
when the other one can function
as a mirror?
When love knocks on the door
to fall in love,
it's needed to put aside
the ugly ego: I am separate
from existence.

Legendary Holi – the festival of colours
linked with Vishnu's Krishna Avatar,
Krishna in Vrindavan, revelled with colours,
merrily celebrating advent of spring
on the day after Holika Dahan.

Holi, pompously observed
with throw of colours
lovingly on each other,
also, as boisterously merry,
"Vasantotsava": cheery spring festival,
"Vasanta", means the spring
and, "Utsava", the festival,
The young and old, rejoicing together,
new harvest festival, the fruitful season,

exhilarating bounties of nature,
enchanting fragrance of different flowers,
exhibiting genuine willingness
to work with each other,

even those with views different,
for "Collective awakening" to happen,
to their benefit,
to the benefit of
community at large.

Divisiveness, a fatal flaw,
manmade climate apocalypse
threatens with extinction,
not just one nation,
nor, a part of the globe,
but, the whole of the Universe.

The spectre of global extinction
looming large,
"this is" an urgent call,
for collective action
involving not merely,
separate nations, or entities,
but, the whole of humankind.

Everyone, is a piece of globe,
which includes all,
excludes none;
Anyone's death diminishes
vast size of humanity.

Burning of helpless widows
on their husband's pyre
community endorsed,
religious doctrine "Sati",
An abhorrent cruel practice.

In this day, digital age
Conventions outdated,
of earlier period in culture
do govern some parts of India.

Our's a male dominated
Social order, with descent
reckoned through male line,
influence of science, technology,
cultivation of scientific temper
penetrate slowly into remote areas,
authoritarian edicts control
concerned religious communities,
the patriarchs decide
essential religious practices
And, followers haven't have
Freedom to dissent,
Punishment meted out to dissenters
At their behest.

Preposterously enough
the Indian women not allowed
to visit cremation ground
to participate in funeral rites,
to say final goodbye
to their dearest ones who
might have spent tens of winters,
tens of summers together
the dearest who departs this life
may be her son, husband, daughter,
her father or mother,
the women forbidden to carry

earthen pot containing holy water
and lead funeral procession
to destination crematorium,
traditionally duty to be assigned to
a male person of the concerned family.
The drill that marks the Hindu funeral
observed exclusively as a male prerogative.
Existing conceptions of religious faith
debar women from conducting funeral rites,
from honouring memory of the loved one
who departs this life.

Archaic conventions cause exclusion of females
impairing their dignity,
underestimating their roles
largely in social sphere,
undermining Constitution's overarching
values of equality, rationality, justice,

The traditional practices iterate,
none but one's son only
rightful successor to conduct last rites
of his father for salvation
of exiting immortal soul;
no son, no salvation of soul!

Instances galore: Women being discarded
for inability to bear a son
to light his father's pyre,
women committed suicide out of shame
for this very same reason.
This has to stop,
shackles of patriarchy to be broken,
the people to be sensitised,
in the greater interest of
the country, and its culture.

Universal phenomena in its totality:
a grand partnership mechanism;
every tiny part of it, essentially important,
to contribute to greater whole for functionality,
Historical relation evolved overtime
between humans and non-humans
pretty well confirms how closely
these two species are intertwined;
their natural close partnership shapes
the grand opera of human civilization;
doubtless, there exists a distinct
cultural, emotive dimension
to this harmonious partnership.

Partnering of female folk
in building a harmonious "Whole",
from the tiny family unit,
to that of larger social network,
rightly eulogised, hence, integral, inseparable
essential for international amity and order.

A woman manifests as love, beauty, kindness
nonviolence, valour, justice, harmony,
responsive to loveful growth of humankind.

GENDER BIAS

In Indian homes
mothers, grandmothers
eagerly serve food,
first to endeared
sons-the advantaged males
then, next to the daughters
painstaking, care-giving females
these aren't isolated incidents
they're daily lessons
in inequality,
the distorting gender bias.
Bias, never strikes a balance
distorts home harmony,
legitimises male entitlement, subtly.

There are umpteen
Government sponsored schemes
to empower women and girls,
policies enacted for girls
in schools, upskilling institutions
enticingly attractive,
policy programmes to sensitise parents
how to bring up children,
but, in everyday practice

girls are denied access
in social fora, homes, workplaces.

What, once, emphatically preached
as proactive measures taken,
to uplift marginalised
economically weaker growing girls
are contradicted conveniently,
what are being practised on ground
in homes, communities, schools;
gender bias deeply ingrained
in everyday living.

Girls never thrive on
government schemes alone
they do deserve
conducive environment
at home, in society
in their educational institutions,

in various training centres
to grow and to raise
to higher positions,
as individuals
not to murmur
with limited physical,
emotional boundaries.

Brave, intelligent girls struggle,
fight with parents,
with domineering relations,

ultimately, to come out of
rigid boundaries
of decelerating existing norms
that block women's upward mobility,
to shape up career trajectory;
ambitions striving girls
always win and succeed,
achieve goals with flying colours,
breaking obstructive shackles,
erasing impeding bias
confidently navigating
enigmatic roadways of life.

Biased practice,
that boys deserve more patronage,
more parental care,
more freedom, more privileges
simply for being boys
than that of girls,
born for being care-giving wives,
caring mother,
being discarded, being obsolete,
has to stop for all days to come.

Women born, not to stay silent,
not told to adjust,
they are empowered to exist,
women can't be allowed
to live in fear.

India emerging fast,
Growing as major economy,
Indian daughters have to
Play their parts,
in this great mission,
women and girls
have to have free access
can't be ignored anymore.

Parents have primary
roles to play,
in raising growing children
gender hierarchy, caste considerations
override impact of
school, and higher education,
girls ignored, excluded
from family decisions
about their marriage,
obsolete norms followed
by parents, subtly impede
cognitive growth of growing girls.

Parents need group sensitisation,
in communities, clubs,
to reshape, sharpen their mindset.

India rising fast as a major economy,
India needs confident daughters,
compassionate sons to contribute
to the great journey
of making India a global leader,

to push forward our nation
unshaken, unscared for, more forceful.

India's skilled youth force,
Women, girls, inclusive,
its strength; its capital;
its growth, unstoppable
India evolves fast to become
a developed nation, a global leader.

SEX RACKET

Women held high
in Indian Culture,
millennial tradition,
its rich civilization.

Despite, a glorious background,
fast developing economy,
Indian women occupying
top positions,
inside and abroad,
women surpassing men
in discharge of duty,
susceptible young women
seduced as sex-commodity
by women racketeers
to organised sex-racket,
a commercial criminal act,
to obtain money
by dishonest, wrong means.

Love brokers engaged
attracting gullible customers
to such rackets,
earn substantial brokerage,
sex-racketeering thrives.

Sex-rackets abound
in populous metropolis,
rich cities, and towns.

This sends shivers
down my spine;
women stoop to
heinous crimes,
 of this type,
agreeably extending
helping hands.

Defying existing
moral, legal forces,
men, to satisfy their
libidinal impulses,
instantly fall prey
to such unlawful
criminal, commercial acts.

Conscience to be
awakened,
police supervision,
legal systems
to operate,
to sensitise barbarous,
brutal persons,
behind clandestine business,
of this nature,
authorities to play
prominent role,
to curb such
criminal operations.

Country like India,
ought not to be
reduced to
a ridiculous level,
India's sanctity destroyed.

Sex is a sweet relationship,
a private act
between the two,
should never cause
moral imbalance,
ought not decimate values
Indian culture
deems sacred.

India honours, extols,
prioritizes women,
precious creation of
the supreme creator,
created to balance
the dynamic nature.

Every woman "Avatar",
descent of God to earth
in bodily form,
as caring mother,
life's co-traveller
loving wife,
ancestor, stand by
daughter/sister
all duty bound,
work assigned

before birth,
to maintain
nature's equilibrium;
Indians unequivocally
confess;
if women rise
India rises,
the world rises,
the humanity becomes
wise, civil, loving, prosperous.

A woman nurtures,
axis of the model family,
stands solidly behind
a man loving a woman.

A woman as mother
has a special place,
in Indian way of life;
mother's care is divine,
selfless, there's no
substitute for a mother.

A woman may
evoke sensuality,
her beauty
embodies spirituality
in sensual form,
Indic civilization
worships women.

EMPOWERING WOMEN

Patriarchal narratives
perilously have distorted
dignity, power, and freedom
of God's creation, women,
who embody
the essence of existence, Shakti.
Unobliging narrow mindset
callously restricts
deserving roles of women
In male dominated societies.
centuries old patriarchal distortions
overshadow women's sovereignty,
relegating socio-spiritual recognition
to the extreme margins.
Patriarchy a poisonous collective ignorance
thrives well on the degradation
and erasure of women.

Prolonged exploitative systems
one day, bound to be annihilated,
its complete overcoming, only helps
evolve socio-spiritual awakening
to arouse, sensitive millions of
aspiring women, equal co-travellers,

with men, on way forward
to liberty, prosperity and happiness.

In collective strength lies
tremendous positive force
to help forward
balance, equality, unity,
most essential intrinsic part of
happy, prosperous, ambitious Universe.

Workload of care giving,
house maintenance, restlessly heavy,
on pliable Indian women

across all levels,
as primary in-charge of kitchen,
job of wearisome, unpaid
house-keeping, child rearing,
burdened with daily timebound assignment
women, rarely are admired or complimented
on the contrary, they are forced on
a hyper-alert-state of stress
causing mayhem in head.

There's on earth
the human existence,
because of women's
loving grace;
from a woman, a man is born,
a king is born, a prophet born,
a leader is born, also, a woman born,

without women,
there would be no one at all.

Divinity, higher knowledge,
accessible to all in the universe,
divine consciousness
transcends the boundaries
of space and time,
all pervasive "absolute reality"
doesn't discriminate between genders,
obstinate, ignorant humans,
seek to limit women's roles;
women are not just mothers,
wives, and daughters,
but are creators of leaders,
warriors, spiritual monks who shape
very essence of
affluent, safe, habitable humanity.

Principle of oneness and equality
derived from the "cosmic unity"
of all beings;
therefore, all in the universe,
are interconnected
at sub-atomic stage.

It's not an axiom,
a well-known cosmic justice of
cosmic unity of all beings.

The countries embracing
gender diversity in
decision making process
tangibly witnessed
improved economic performance,
women leaders' willing entry
into power politics
better women participation
in developmental projects,
inclusive workplace policies,
enhanced social uplift,
fostering a culture of
fairness and equity.

G20 under India's leadership
in two thousand and twenty-three,
successfully signalled,
world leaders' increasing recognition,
to promote equal, effective, meaningful
participation of women
in the economy
as decision makers.

Women-led development
approach lovingly leads to
gender diversity,
socio-economic empowerment,
guaranteeing
a bright, warless, harmonious world.

Acknowledgement

I owe a debt of gratitude to "Black Eagle Books" – a non-profit publisher established to propagate literature of India – at Dublin (USA), Bhubaneswar (India) for gracefully agreeing to publish the collection of poems, **"INDIA FOR THE WORLD"** and deliver the published, well-designed book on time.

I must thank Mr. Satya Patnaik (USA) and Mr. Ashok Parida (India) for timely help bring the book to life – capturing Indian spirits appealing to all ages. With beautifully designed cover, collection of poems **"INDIA FOR THE WORLD"**, I hope, will be appreciated, read and cherished.

I shall treasure the limitless love that Prof. Prafulla Kumar Mohanty has shown to me, for all days to come. He is an erudite scholar, inspiring teacher, visionary administrator, poet essayist, critic, National Academy Award Winner in literature, retired professor in English, at present writing reflective essays. Despite very busy schedule, he analysed all my poems and has written "Foreword" for the book **"INDIA FOR THE WORLD"**. I am indebted to him.

I shall be failing in my duty if I don't appreciate herculean task of making analysis of all my poems, performed by my closest friend, guide, Prof. Manmatha Kundu – an internationally reputed ELT expert, poet, novelist, and inspiring teacher. He is a former Director of Tribal Language and Culture, former visiting Professor of Hudaida University (Republic of Yemen). He has taken pains to write the "Preface: a reader's response" for the book **"INDIA FOR THE WORLD"**. I express my gratitude to him.

I owe a debt of gratitude to Prof. Arun Kumar Mohanty – a renowned professor in English, visionary administrator, acclaimed editor of "Odisha Review" – Odisha Govt's official journal, who has very kindly written "Afterword" (Epilogue) for **"INDIA FOR THE WORLD"**. I pay my regards to him. He stands solidly behind me.

A special mention must be made here for Dr. Alekha Chandra Padhiary, former Indian Administrative Service Cadre Officer, erudite scholar, poet, inspiring speaker, a research scholar on Jagannath Culture, writer of repute, who stands behind me in pleasure, and penury. I am indebted to him for his constant advice.

Shri Jogendra Mullick, a commoner belonging to my locality is an ideal for many. He rose by dint of labour and patience, from a very humble beginning to a hotelier, earning his bread and butter comfortably well, with a happy family. I love him too.

A lot of thanks to Mr. Sabyasachi Mishra, proprietor of "VIRTUAL IMAGES" who has since beginning, has typed out my poems and has emailed a few of them to "Odisha Review" for publication. I express my gratitude to him.

Ajit Kumar Mahapatra

Afterword

Arun Kumar Mohanty

I had an opportunity of going through a few poems written by Ajit Kumar Mahapatra and included in his second collection of poems titled *India for the World*. These poems, based on his real life experiences, portray his vision of life which is shaped by the land he lives in and the people he has interacted with over a period of more than half a century.

Mahapatra'a poems, like those of most Indian poets in English, are rooted in Indian tradition and culture, which is diverse and which bears the essence of unity in diversity. However, it is not always the same cultural tradition, the same set of customs and rituals that is depicted in the poems of all Indian poets in English who hail from different backgrounds living in different parts of the country. Nissim Ezekiel was born to a Marathi-speaking Bene Israel Jewish family in Mumbai. A.K. Ramanujan was born to a South Indian family in Mysore, who received his education in India before moving to the United States. Jayanta Mahapatra, who was born to a Christian family in Cuttack and spent most of his time in the same city, once observed: "I don't think there is one India; Odisha is one India, Bengal is another. Maharashtra, Kerala, Kashmir—all these are different Indias. It is easier to relate yourself to a particular region than to talk about the whole of India as a construct" (quoted by Gopal Lahiri in the Book Review of *Resonance: English Poetry from Poets of Odisha,* edited by Chittaranjan Misra, Jaydeep Sarangi, Mona Dash (Author Press, 2020), published in *borderlessjournal.com, 2025).*

The poet's native village on the bank of river Subarnarekha in north Odisha serves as the background of two of his poems, "My Native Village" included in this collection and "A Visit to My Village" included in the first collection of his poems. His memory is filled with the "fascinating, picturesque riverscape", chirping birds and low hoarse sounds of flying crows waking up villagers in the morning. He is also reminded of quill pens which students "used for fine [hand] writing during school days." The umbrageous astonishing mango leaves, tall coconut trees, luscious banana plants, lush green wide paddy fields surrounding the village temple would mesmerize all. He treasures the memory of living in a humble mud house, growing together with family and friends. The poet also notices the subtle changes the village is witnessing these days.

India's rich cultural heritage and its religious diversity find eloquent expression in a number of poems included in this collection. A dip at the confluence of the Ganga, Yamuna and Saraswati during the Mahakumbha which is believed to bring about purification of the soul forms the theme of "A

Holy Dip at the Sangam." Similarly, the poem "The Last Rakhi" depicts the sacred bond between brothers and sisters. The significance of Holi, the festival of colours, is highlighted in "Holi Revelry". Nuakhai, an important agricultural festival observed mostly in western Odisha, finds powerful expression in the poem "Nuakhai Festival". The poet also describes the way Christmas is celebrated in India. The celebrations are not confined to the Christian community; it pervades the entire society. The birth of Lord Christ is also celebrated with pomp by the people who celebrate the birth of Lord Krishna.

Poverty, hunger and suffering constitute the theme of several works of Indian literature including Indian poetry in English. It is natural that the poems of Ajit Kumar Mahapatra depict this grim reality. The poem "Sunken Eyes" depicts the predicament of a woman in her fifties, thirsty and hungry, as one alights from a city bus. This is a sight which is not unfamiliar at a busy bus stop like Rajmahal Square in Bhubaneswar or elsewhere. At almost every bus stop, one meets such hungry faces, some begging for alms and a few not expressing it in so many words. The protagonist here is deeply moved by the emaciated look of the woman under the hot sun, her sunken eyes and shrunk cheeks. Instead of ignoring her as most people do, he pauses there awhile, offers her water from the water bottle he carries; takes her to a hotel on the pavement and orders food for her, which she gratefully takes. After eating the meal, she does not forget to offer him the blessing of a long life—"May you live long, till ripe old age." Abject poverty has not robbed her of a sense of gratitude to the man who has tried to relieve her of her suffering by offering her a little water and some food.

The poem reminds us of another face of hunger depicted in the celebrated poet Jayanta Mahapatra's poem, "Hunger." The hunger there symbolizes the poverty of a fisherman and his daughter, and also the sexual desires of the customer who comes there to gratify his desire. The fisherman does not hesitate to trade his own daughter for money and the daughter herself has no inhibition in obliging her father and the customer.

I heard him say: My daughter, she's just turned fifteen.. Feel her. I'll be back soon, your bus leaves at nine. ("Hunger")

The poem "Hunger" brings out a murky, dirty picture of poverty driving man to commit an ugly and immoral act of offering his daughter's body for sex in exchange of money, while the poem "Sunken Eyes" reveals the kindness and generosity of both the protagonist and the woman he comes across.

Unlike another well-known name in Indian poetry in English Niranjan Mohanty, Ajit Kumar Mahapatra does not have to travel to Kalahandi, to discover the sordid face of poverty: "Perhaps, the hearts go heavier here/ by day, and the bodies, by night, lonelier./ Cattle chew paper scraps and linen/ butterflies flounder about black stones./ Rivers do not flow here. The pools/ and wells never glow with the bliss of water/ no vegetation, no fruition/ only the bones; hunger seeks an ascension. ("Kalahandi"). In Mahapatra's poem, poverty presents itself, not in remote Kalahandi, but in the busy streets of a so-called smart city.

The poet is very much aware of the evils of society. He is deeply conscious of the gender bias prevailing in our villages and towns. He knows, patriarchal narratives have perilously distorted the dignity, power and freedom of women. In spite of government schemes to bring about parity, "in everyday practice/ girls are denied access/ in social fora, homes, workplaces." Probably incidents of burning of the girl child and bids of immolation by young women at several places in our country are in his mind. The poet's ultimate message is: "women can't be allowed/to live in fear." All these social evils have not blurred the poet's vision of a healthy society. He draws inspiration from the concept of *vasudhaiva kutukbakam*, and considers the world as a family. He is inspired by the doctrine of peace and non-violence and sees how India would lead the nations on the path of love and peace.

Black Eagle Books

www.blackeaglebooks.org
info@blackeaglebooks.org

Black Eagle Books, an independent publisher, was founded as a nonprofit organization in April, 2019. It is our mission to connect and engage the Indian diaspora and the world at large with the best of works of world literature published on a collaborative platform, with special emphasis on foregrounding Contemporary Classics and New Writing.

www.ingramcontent.com/pod-product-compliance
Lightning Source LLC
Chambersburg PA
CBHW060614080526
44585CB00013B/824